Peterson Field Guides®
For Young Naturalists

Birds of Prey

Jonathan P. Latimer
Karen Stray Nolting

Illustrations by Roger Tory Peterson

Foreword by Virginia Marie Peterson

Houghton Mifflin Company
Boston 1999

FOREWORD

My husband, Roger Tory Peterson, traced his interest in nature back to an encounter he had with an exhausted flicker when he was only 11 years old. When he found what he thought was a dead bird in a bundle of brown feathers, he touched it and the bird suddenly exploded into life, showing its golden feathers. Roger said it was "like resurrection." That experience was "the crucial moment" that started Roger on a lifelong journey with nature. He combined his passion for nature with his talent as an artist to create a series of field guides and paintings that changed the way people experience the natural world. Roger often spoke of an even larger goal, however. He believed that an understanding of the natural world would lead people — especially young people — to a recognition of "the interconnnectedness of things all over the world." The Peterson Field Guides for Young Naturalists are a continuation of Roger's interest in educating and inspiring young people to see that "life itself is important — not just our-selves, but all life."
                                                      — **Virginia Marie Peterson**

Special thanks to Dick Walton for his expert advice.

Library of Congress Cataloging-in-Publication Data

Latimer, Jonathan P.

Birds of prey / Jonathan P. Latimer & Karen Stray Nolting ; illustrations by Roger Tory Peterson ; fore-word by Virginia Marie Peterson. p.   cm. — (Peterson field guides for young naturalists)

Summary: Describes the physical characteristics, behavior, voices, and habitats of a variety of eagles, hawk, falcons, and owls. Includes Peterson System of identifying birds by their unique markings.

ISBN 0-395-95211-5 (cl). — ISBN 0-395-92277-1 (pbk.)

1. Birds of prey — Juvenile literature. 2. Birds of prey — Identification — Juvenile literature. [1. Birds of prey.] I. Nolting, Karen Stray. II. Peterson, Roger Tory, 1908–1996, ill. III. Title. IV. Series.

QL696.F3L37   1999   598.9 — dc21   98-35516 CIP AC

Photo Credits

Bald Eagle: Steve Sherrod; Golden Eagle: Rick Kline; Turkey Vulture: Lee Kuhn; Black Vulture: Christopher Crowley; Osprey: Isidor Jeklin; Red-tailed Hawk: Christopher Crowley; Northern Goshawk: Rick Kline; Northern Harrier: Frank Schleicher; Peregrine Falcon: James Weaver; Cooper's Hawk: Rick Kline; Sharp-shinned Hawk: Isidor Jeklin; Merlin: John Heidecker; American Kestrel: Rick Kline; Great Horned Owl: Gijsbert van Frankenhuyzen; Snowy Owl: Mike Hopiak; Common Barn Owl: B. B. Hall; Short-eared Owl: James Weaver; Long-eared Owl: J. Hough; Eastern Screech Owl: Mike Hopiak.

Book design by Lisa Diercks. Typeset in Mrs Eaves and Base 9 from Emigre

Manufactured in the United States of America

WOZ 10 9 8 7 6 5 4 3 2 1

CONTENTS

HOW TO WATCH
BIRDS OF PREY

No other birds have been more admired — and more feared — than birds of prey. Swift and often silent, they are the hunters of the bird world, pursuing animals, reptiles, insects, and sometimes other birds.

Many of the fascinating birds of prey that live in North America can be found in this book. It is divided into four sections. Each section is arranged according to the size of the bird of prey, beginning with the largest and ending with the smallest. To many people, birds of prey means large birds, like eagles or hawks. But some birds of prey are small. Merlins are about the size of a pigeon, and American Kestrels are even smaller.

The illustrations in this book were painted by Roger Tory Peterson, the man who revolutionized bird identification. He invented a simple system of drawings and pointers (now known as the "Peterson System") that call attention to the unique marks on each kind of bird. This book introduces the Peterson System to beginners and young birders. It can help you answer the most important question of all: *What bird of prey is that?*

What Bird of Prey Is That?

It is often difficult to get close enough to a bird of prey to see it clearly. Many times you will see it only when it is flying overhead. The illustrations on pages 46 and 47 of this book will help you identify birds of prey in flight.

There are also a number of questions you can ask yourself about the bird you see. You may not be able to answer them all, but the answers you do find may give you the clues you need to identify the bird.

What Color Is the Bird?

Color is usually one of the first things you notice when you see a bird. But it is often difficult to tell the color of a bird of prey, especially when you are looking up into the bright sky. To make matters worse, many birds of prey are brown or black and look similar to each other. But the good news is that the feathers of birds of prey do have patterns that can help you identify them. For example, the wings of an Osprey have black patches. An adult Bald Eagle has a white head and tail. These are called field marks.

Does It Have Any Field Marks?

Field marks are found on a bird's head, wings, body, or tail. They can help you recognize a bird at a distance. For example, when you see a large black bird soaring overhead, you may notice that the back edges of its wings are lighter colored than the front. If that is so, you will know right away that it is a Turkey Vulture.

What Is a Bird of Prey?

Birds of prey include eagles, hawks, ospreys, falcons, vultures, and owls. What makes them birds of prey is the fact that they have curved bills and strong feet with talons, and they eat meat. Most birds of prey also strike their target while flying, catching some prey in the air and other prey on the ground. Some even grab their prey off branches of trees or bushes.

How Does It Fly? Except for owls, you are most likely to see birds of prey when they are flying during the day. How they fly can give you an excellent clue to what kind of bird they are. Red-tailed Hawks soar and wheel high in the sky. Turkey Vultures also soar, but they hold their wings in a slight V-shape.

What Is Its Shape? Shape is another clue to identifying a bird of prey. Does it have sharply pointed wings and a long tail? Then it may be a falcon. Does it have broad wings and a rounded tail? Then it may be a hawk.

What Is the Bird Doing? As you watch birds of prey you may notice that they behave in certain ways. Some of these behaviors are good clues to the bird's identity. If you see a small bird of prey hovering over a spot with rapid wingbeats, it is probably an American Kestrel.

Migration

Many birds of prey migrate north in spring to their nesting areas and south in fall to warmer areas where there is more food. They often fly during the day, following the same migration route each year. In fall hundreds of birds of prey pass over places such as Cape May, New Jersey, and Hawk Mountain Sanctuary in Pennsylvania. Watching these birds has become popular, and many people visit these sites during migration.

Where Did You See the Bird of Prey? It is easy to understand that you are more likely to find some birds in certain places. Bald Eagles and Ospreys, which eat fish, are usually found near water or at the seashore. Golden Eagles are found in open country. But birds can fly anywhere. You may see a Bald Eagle a long way from water or a Golden Eagle near a lake. So keep your eyes open. An unexpected bird can turn up wherever you are.

What Does It Sound Like? Most birds of prey are quiet, but the high, squealing *kreeeeee* of a Red-tailed Hawk is unmistakable. And you will never forget the *Hoo, hoo-oo, hoo, hoo* of a Great Horned Owl.

BALD EAGLE

The Bald Eagle is the national bird of the United States. It has a powerful and majestic appearance. Its wing span is over 7 feet. This bird is considered sacred by many Native Americans.

The Bald Eagle often hunts by sitting on a high perch above water, looking for fish. When it spots something, it swoops down to catch it in its sharp talons.

For many years the population of Bald Eagles dwindled because of hunting and the use of the pesticide DDT. When the hunting of Bald Eagles was made illegal and the use of DDT was banned, the population of Bald Eagles began to recover. Today there are more than 15,000 Bald Eagles in Alaska and nearly 10,000 in the lower 48 states.

Did You Know?

- The design for the Great Seal of the United States was selected in 1782. The Bald Eagle appears on the front side of the seal. The Eagle holds the arrows of war and the olive branch of peace in its talons. You can find the seal on the one-dollar bill.
- The Bald Eagle's nest is the largest built by a single pair of birds in North America. One nest weighed more than 2 tons.
- The Bald Eagle is found only in North America.

Yellow eyes

Large yellow bill

White head

Dark head
with dark eyes
and dark bill

(Adult)

White tail
feathers

Males
and
females
look alike.

Dark tail

(Young)

Habitat Bald Eagles usually stay near seacoasts, large rivers, lakes, and swamps where they can find food. During migration they may sometimes be seen near mountains and dry open country, including deserts.

Voice The Bald Eagle's cry is a harsh cackle that may remind you of the cry of a gull. It sounds like *kleek-kik-ik-ik-ik* or a lower *kak-kak-kak.*

Food Bald Eagles usually eat fish, which they catch for themselves or steal from Ospreys. Bald Eagles sometimes eat ducks or other waterfowl and small animals such as squirrels and rabbits. They may also scavenge dead animals.

GOLDEN EAGLE

The striking Golden Eagle is a magnificent flier. It glides and soars through the air, occasionally flapping its wings in unhurried, powerful beats. Sometimes it will circle slowly, spiraling upward until it is a speck in the sky. Golden Eagles also dive after their prey at great speed.

Golden Eagles are good hunters, but they need a large area to hunt in. A nesting pair needs approximately 35 square miles. Pairs of Golden Eagles sometimes hunt as a team. The second eagle catches the prey that escapes the first.

For years farmers and sheepherders hunted Golden Eagles because they sometimes preyed on young animals. The population of Golden Eagles declined alarmingly. Then studies found that worries about eagles taking young animals were exaggerated. The hunting of Golden Eagles was banned in 1962. Today the population of Golden Eagles is thought to be stable. It is estimated that there are 4,000 to 5,000 pairs in the lower 48 states.

Patch of gold
feathers on neck

Bands on tail
less visible

(Young)

(Adult)

White at base of tail

Habitat Golden Eagles
are most often found in
open areas, especially near
foothills and mountains.

Voice Golden Eagles
make a sound like a bark,
but it is seldom heard.

Food Golden Eagles
hunt mostly small animals such as squirrels, prairie
dogs, and jackrabbits. They may hunt smaller animals
such as mice and small birds. They are also known to
hunt much larger animals including foxes, antelopes,
deer, owls, and cranes.

Did You Know?
- The Golden Eagle is the second-largest eagle in North America, after the Bald Eagle.
- The dives of Golden Eagles have been measured at 200 miles per hour.
- Golden Eagles return to the same nesting sites year after year.

TURKEY VULTURE

Cartoons sometimes show buzzards or vultures circling above characters lost in the desert, waiting for them to die. In real life, vultures eat animals only after they are dead. By doing this, they help keep the environment clean and reduce the spread of diseases.

The black shape of a Turkey Vulture is usually seen as it soars high overhead, riding the air currents. Several vultures often circle slowly, lazily flapping their wings. They are easy to recognize because their wings have a touch of white on the back edges. When they fly, vultures sometimes rock back and forth as they tilt and sway in the wind. When a Turkey Vulture sees food, it circles downward. If other vultures see this happening, they circle in to join the meal.

Did You Know?
- Turkey Vultures find their prey by smell — which is unusual for birds — as well as by sight.
- Fossils of vultures have been found in North America dating back 65 million years.
- The name of the Turkey Vulture comes from its featherless head, which reminded people of a turkey's head. Turkey Vultures are sometimes known as buzzards.

Turkey Vultures soar with their wings lifted in a flat V-shape. They can soar to 4,000 feet or more.

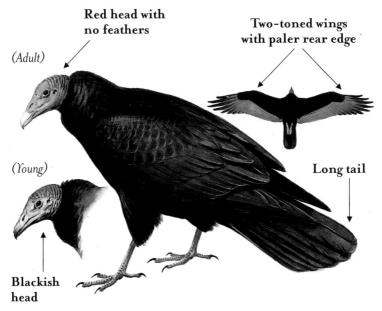

Red head with no feathers

(Adult)

Two-toned wings with paler rear edge

(Young)

Long tail

Blackish head

Males and females look alike.

Habitat Turkey Vultures are usually seen in the air over open country, woods, deserts, and foothills. They sometimes perch on dead trees or fence posts.

Voice Turkey Vultures are rarely heard. They sometimes hiss at each other, or grunt or growl.

Food Turkey Vultures feed mostly on dead animals. Sometimes they eat insects or fish or even vegetable matter.

BLACK VULTURE

Vultures may not appear to be very attractive, but they perform a very useful service in the wild. They scavenge dead animals and garbage. This helps prevent the spread of disease and keeps the landscape clean.

Like their larger relative, the Turkey Vulture, Black Vultures circle in the air, looking for food. But Turkey Vultures often soar alone, while Black Vultures are seen in flocks. Black Vultures have stubbier tails and shorter, wider wings than Turkey Vultures. Black Vultures are also more aggressive than Turkey Vultures and sometimes drive them away from food.

Did You Know?
- Turkey Vultures can find food by smell, but Black Vultures cannot. They find their food by sight.
- Black Vultures are less afraid of people than most large birds are. In the Caribbean and Mexico, they are often seen walking around town markets or harbors, looking for scraps.

Black Vultures flap their wings and glide
for a short distance, then flap again.

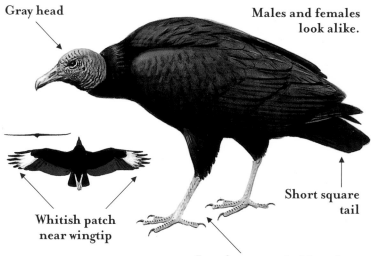

Gray head

Males and females
look alike.

Whitish patch
near wingtip

Short square
tail

Legs longer and whiter than
Turkey Vulture's

Habitat Flocks of Black Vultures are usually seen in
the air over flat lowlands such as the plains along the
ocean coast. They spend the night in forests, where they
also nest.

Voice Black Vultures are usually silent, but they sometimes hiss, grunt, or make barking sounds at each other
when fighting over food.

Food Black Vultures feed mostly on dead animals,
especially near city dumps, slaughterhouses, and along
highways. They sometimes catch small birds and animals.
They will also eat eggs or rotten fruit and vegetables.

OSPREY

The Osprey is the only bird of prey that hunts by diving into the water. Usually an osprey will cruise about 100 feet above the water. When it spots a fish near the surface, it may hover in the air, waiting for the right moment, or it may dive straight down. The Osprey plunges into the water feet-first. If it catches a fish, it grips it with the long talons on both feet and flies upward. As it flies, the osprey holds the fish so that its head points forward. This reduces the resistance of the air and makes flying easier.

Ospreys often chose a tall tree or other high spot near water for their nest. Both parents build the nest out of sticks and line it with soft material. The same nesting site may be added to year after year, eventually becoming a huge pile of sticks. In many places people build platforms on poles for Ospreys to use as nesting sites. This is often a successful way to attract Ospreys to an area.

Males and females look alike.

Nest high in tree

Hovers before diving feet-first on prey

Dark patch at bend in wings

White head

Wide black patch on cheek

Dark wings

Wings held at sharp angle

White chest

(Adult)

Habitat Ospreys live along seacoasts, rivers, and lakes where large numbers of fish are found. They can also be seen around marshes and reservoirs.

Did You Know?
- Bald Eagles sometimes steal fish from Ospreys by chasing them and making them drop their catch.
- The Osprey is also called a Fish Hawk.

Voice Ospreys make a series of sharp whistles that sound like *cheep, cheep* or *yewk, yewk*. Near the nest the call is a furious *cheereek!*

Food Ospreys eat all kinds of fish. They also some-times eat snakes, frogs, and birds.

RED-TAILED HAWK

Red-tailed Hawks have amazing eyesight. They can see two to three times better than we can. They will sit for hours on a high perch looking for small animals. When they see one, they take off with powerful wingbeats. Then they swoop down and catch their prey with their talons. Young Red-tailed Hawks often hunt by flying over fields.

Red-tailed Hawks are North America's most common hawk. They can be seen almost anywhere, sailing overhead or perched in high places along roads. They hunt rodents and other small animals and play a big part in controlling their numbers.

Red-tailed Hawks mate for life. Often the pair will stay in the same area all year but change their nesting site. Some pairs use the same nesting sites every other year. Young hawks tend to migrate great distances before settling down in one place.

Did You Know?
- Adult Red-tailed Hawks stay away from humans but will swoop and scream at intruders who come too close to their nests.

RED-TAILED HAWK

The colors of Red-tailed Hawks vary in different regions.

Red tail

When perched, Red-tailed Hawks have a stocky build and wide tail.

White chest

(Young)

(Adult)

Tail red on top, pale underneath

Males and females look alike.

No red tail on young

Habitat Red-tailed Hawks live in open country, woodlands, mountains, and plains. They are often seen sitting in trees or on fences or telephone poles along roads.

Voice The call of a Red-tailed is a high squealing *kreeeeee* that slurs downward. They also make a hissing sound.

Food Red-tailed Hawks eat whatever is available where they live. They eat small mammals, birds, and reptiles.

NORTHERN GOSHAWK

This powerful hunter of the northern woods often climbs from branch to branch, keeping watch for prey. When a Northern Goshawk spots something, it can fly with surprising speed. Its long tail and rounded wings help it turn sharply to avoid hitting trees or bushes. It may even chase its prey on the ground into thick under-brush. Goshawks have also been known to run into buildings to catch a chicken or to wade into shallow water after a duck.

Northern Goshawks mate for life, but live alone except during nesting season. While a pair is building their nest, they often make soaring flights together. The male dives at the female from above the trees. Then both birds — sometimes only a few feet apart — fly slowly through the trees. Other times they move far apart and make spectac-ular dives toward each other.

Northern Goshawks can be almost fearless. They have been known to attack chickens even when people are standing nearby. They have also tried to carry away wood-en duck decoys.

Males and females look alike.

Black crown on head

Broad white stripe over eye

White bar over eye

Black cheeks

(Young)

Brown stripes on both chest and belly

Pale gray chest with thin black bars

Long tail ⟶

Bands on tail

Habitat Northern Goshawks are usually found in forests, especially in the mountains.

Voice The call of the Northern Goshawk is a harsh *kak, kak, kak* or *kuk, kuk, kuk.*

Food Northern Goshawks hunt larger birds, such as crows and ducks, and small mammals, such as rabbits and squirrels. They also hunt small birds, mice, chipmunks, snakes, and insects.

Did You Know?
• It is very dangerous to go near any hawk's nest. Female Northern Goshawks are especially fierce when protecting their nest. They have been known to injure people who come too close.
• The name "Goshawk" is short for "goose hawk," which is what this bird was originally called in Europe.

NORTHERN HARRIER

The Northern Harrier is a large, slender hawk with long slim wings and a long tail. You can recognize it by a white patch at the base of its tail and black wing-tips, which look like they have been dipped in ink.

A Northern Harrier is usually seen over marshes, gliding with its wings held in a shallow V. It flies back and forth with a tilting motion, searching the ground for food. Like owls, a Northern Harrier hunts by sound as well as by sight. When it finds its prey, it drops on it suddenly, taking it by surprise.

Pairs of Northern Harriers divide the work of feeding their young in an unusual way. The male does most of the hunting. He drops the food near the nest and then flies on. The female picks up the food and feeds it to the young.

Did You Know?
• Northern Harriers will drive crows, hawks, and even eagles away from their nesting site.
• Northern Harriers are known to hover near prairie fires, catching the small animals that are driven into the open by the flames.
• The Northern Harrier is also called the Marsh Hawk.

NORTHERN HARRIER

Brown back

When Northern Harriers hunt, their wings are held in a flat V-shape.

(Young)

Reddish Chest

Pale gray

White patch at base of tail

Dark wing tips

(Adult male)

(Adult female)

Brown with streaks on chest

Habitat Northern Harriers are found throughout all of North America. They hunt in fields, marshes, prairies, meadows, and other open grasslands.

Voice The Northern Harrier is usually silent, but at its nest it utters a weak call that sounds like *pee, pee, pee* or a sharp whistle.

Food Depending on what is available, Northern Harriers eat small mammals, birds, and sometimes frogs, snakes, lizards, or insects. Some seem to specialize in hunting rats, voles, and other rodents.

PEREGRINE FALCON

Few birds fly as fast as the Peregrine Falcon. It hunts by soaring high in the sky and scanning the air for birds. When a Peregrine sees a bird below, it turns downward and gives a few quick beats of its wings. Then it folds its wings close to its body and dives at up to 200 miles per hour. The Peregrine Falcon overtakes its prey and strikes it with a tremendous blow with both feet. If the bird dodges out of the way, the Peregrine flies back up and tries again.

Peregrine Falcons are found in most parts of the world, but once they almost disappeared from North America. Pesticides such as DDT caused Peregrines to lay eggs with shells so thin that they often broke during incubation. By the mid-1970s, Peregrines had disappeared from the eastern United States, and their number was reduced by 80 to 90 percent in the West.

Following the ban of DDT in 1972, scientists began raising young Peregrine Falcons in captivity and releasing them into the wild. This has been very successful. By 1991, more than 4,000 Peregrines had been released. The Peregrine Falcon has now been taken off the list of endangered species.

PEREGRINE FALCON

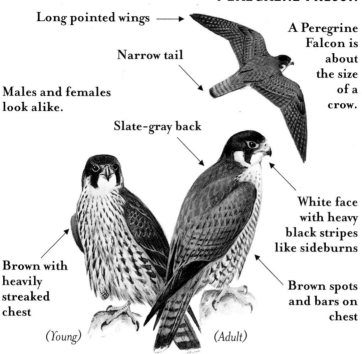

Long pointed wings ⟶

Narrow tail

A Peregrine Falcon is about the size of a crow.

Males and females look alike.

Slate-gray back

White face with heavy black stripes like sideburns

Brown with heavily streaked chest

Brown spots and bars on chest

(Young)   *(Adult)*

Habitat Peregrines hunt in open fields and country-side, near mountains, and along seacoasts.

Voice Peregrines call with a rapid *kek kek kek kek* sound when flying. Around the nest they make a repeated *we'chew, we'chew.*

Food Peregrines hunt a wide variety of birds. In cities they catch pigeons and starlings. In the country they hunt ducks and shorebirds, gulls, and even small songbirds.

Did You Know?

• Most Peregrine Falcons dig a shallow hole in gravel on a cliff ledge for their nest. But some Peregrines have used skyscraper ledges, tall towers, and bridges for their nesting sites.
• The name "Peregrine" comes from a Latin word meaning traveler or wanderer.

COOPER'S HAWK

Cooper's Hawks sneak up on their prey. They move quietly from branch to branch, listening and watching. When they get close enough, they fly out swiftly and catch the prey with their talons. Sometimes Cooper's Hawks fly low over the ground, using trees or brush for cover. Then they accelerate and surprise their prey in the air or on the ground.

The short wings and long tail of Cooper's Hawks make them very good at maneuvering through woods. They can fly fast and turn quickly when they need to.

Cooper's Hawks sometimes attack crows, but groups of crows will also attack a hawk, especially near the crows' nests. This is called "mobbing," and it usually drives the hawk away.

COOPER'S HAWK

Brown with streaks on chest

Gray back with rust-colored bars on chest

A Cooper's Hawk is about the size of a crow.

(Adult)

(Young)

White on belly

Rounded tail

Long tail with rounded tip

Males and females look alike, but females are larger.

Habitat Cooper's Hawks live in forests, woods, and farmland. They use tall trees for nesting sites and hunt in woods and brush.

Voice Cooper's Hawks make a rapid *kek, kek, kek* sound near their nests.

Food Cooper's Hawks eat other birds, including starlings, jays, robins, doves, and quail. They also hunt small mammals, such as chipmunks and squirrels, and sometimes even snakes, lizards, and frogs.

Did You Know?

- Cooper's Hawks can fly up to 55 miles per hour.
- Cooper's Hawks are known to hunt quails by sound rather than sight.

27

SHARP-SHINNED HAWK

Sharp-shinned Hawks, or "Sharpies," are the smallest of the hawks that hunt birds. They are very good fliers, able to twist and turn through thick woods. Sharpies can dart low over the ground, weaving through the underbrush, then turn abruptly to catch their prey. They also perch in dense thickets and wait for birds to approach. When a bird comes near, the hawk rushes out and catches its surprised prey.

Sharp-shinned Hawks are often confused with Cooper's Hawks, even by experts. They have similar markings, but Cooper's Hawks are larger and have a rounded tail. An adult Sharp-shinned Hawk is about the same size as a jay. A Cooper's Hawk is about the size of a crow. Although they live in the same areas, there are many more Sharp-shinned Hawks than Cooper's Hawks, though the number of Sharpies may be declining.

Sharp-shinned Hawks migrate in large groups along seacoasts, the shores of lakes, or the edges of mountain ranges in fall and spring. Some Sharpies migrate as far south as Panama.

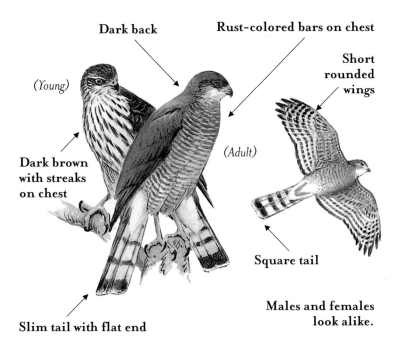

Dark back

Rust-colored bars on chest

Short rounded wings

(Young)

Dark brown with streaks on chest

(Adult)

Square tail

Slim tail with flat end

Males and females look alike.

Habitat Sharp-shinned Hawks live in remote woods or thickets almost anywhere in North America. They are seldom found in open country, except during migration.

Voice The call of a Sharp-shinned Hawk is shrill and rapid. It sounds like *kik–kik–kik.*

Food Sharp-shinned Hawks most often hunt small birds, including sparrows, robins, and doves. Sometimes they also eat rodents, bats, lizards, frogs, grasshoppers, and moths.

Did You Know?
• The color of a Sharp-shinned Hawk's eyes change from yellow to red as it grows older.
• Sharp-shinned Hawks will sometimes raid bird feeders to try to catch small birds.

MERLIN

This small falcon is only about the size of a pigeon, but it is one of the best fliers among the birds of prey. A Merlin is very fast, moving at up to 45 miles per hour in level flight. It is also very active. It catches most of its prey in the air, and its courtship flight is spectacular.

When hunting, Merlins use their speed in two ways. Sometimes they sit on a perch where they can spot their prey. Then they quickly fly out and catch it in the air. Other times they glide low among trees or over open ground. When they spot their prey, they swiftly overtake it, catching it by surprise in midair.

Did You Know?

- Merlins follow the birds they prey on when they migrate south in fall.
- The name Merlin comes from the Old French name for this bird and has nothing to do with the magician in the tales of King Arthur.
- The Merlin was once known as the Pigeon Hawk.

Larger than male

Blue-gray on back and wings

The Merlin is a small compact falcon.

(Female)

(Male)

Brown with black bands on tail

Long tail with black bands

Broad black bands on tail

Females and young look alike.

Habitat Merlins are found in open country and pastures, foothills, and marshes. They can also be found in some cities, particularly those located on the midwestern prairies.

Voice When defending its nest, a Merlin will make a harsh cackling call that sounds like *ki-ki-ki-ki-keee*.

Food Merlins hunt mainly small birds, including sandpipers, doves, jays, and blackbirds. In cities they hunt sparrows and pigeons. They also hunt dragonflies, which they catch and devour while flying.

AMERICAN KESTREL

About the size of a robin, the American Kestrel is the smallest falcon in North America. It is most easily recognized when it is hunting. Kestrels often hover over one place, beating their wings rapidly like a kingfisher. If they don't find anything, they fly to a new location and hover again. When they see their prey, they drop lower, then swoop down on it quickly. Then they carry their prey to a perch to eat it.

Kestrels do most of their hunting in the morning or late afternoon. They usually spend the middle part of the day sitting quietly on a high perch. A kestrel may be seen sitting upright on a telephone wire or in a tree, flicking its tail.

Kestrels have narrow, pointed wings. When they are not hovering, they fly with rapid beats of their wings, and then glide. They are so fast that they can catch their prey in flight.

Did You Know?
- Individual kestrels sometimes hunt only one type of prey.
- Kestrels rarely need to drink water. They get all the liquid they need from the food they eat.
- The American Kestrel used to be known as the Sparrow Hawk.

American Kestrels are about the size of a robin and fly like a swallow.

Pointed wings

Larger than male

Black and white face pattern

(Female)

Long tail

Blue-gray wings

(Male)

No other small hawk has a reddish back or tail.

Habitat Kestrels are found in open country, pastures, deserts, cities, and at the edges of woods or along highways.

Voice When alarmed, a kestrel's call sounds like a high, rapid *klee klee klee* or *killy killy killy.*

Food Kestrels eat many kinds of large insects, such as grasshoppers, crickets, and dragonflies. They also hunt mice, bats, birds, lizards, frogs, and even earthworms. In cities they prey on House Sparrows.

GREAT HORNED OWL

The Great Horned Owl is one of the largest and most powerful of all the North American owls. It is a fearless hunter with excellent hearing and very good vision — even at night. Its large ear tufts, or "horns," give this owl its name. These tufts are visible when an owl is perched, but they flatten out when it flies.

Great Horned Owls watch for prey from a high perch and then swoop down to capture it in their talons. But they also can weave their way through thick branches in a forest at very high speed. When they find their prey, they fold their wings and dive. They keep their wings closed until the very last moment, and by then it is usually too late for their prey. The flight of a Great Horned Owl is so silent that the prey is caught completely by surprise.

The color of the Great Horned Owl varies from region to region. They tend to be paler in the South and darker in the Pacific Northwest.

The horns of the Great Horned Owl are really tufts of feathers.

Males and females look alike.

Large eyes

White throat patch

Dark bars across chest

Habitat Great Horned Owls live in forests and thickets almost everywhere in North America. They can also be found near streams and in open country.

Voice The call of the male is usually four or five hoots: *Hoo, hoo-oo, hoo, hoo.* He is often answered by the female's six or eight hoots that are lower in pitch: *Hoo, hoo-hoo-hoo, hoo-oo, hoo-oo.* The hooting can be heard more than a mile away.

Food Great Horned Owls will eat almost any small animal, including other birds, small mammals such as mice, squirrels, and rabbits, and sometimes fish and insects. Their prey also includes larger birds such as hawks, geese, swans, and turkeys, and animals such as woodchucks and porcupines.

Did You Know?

- The soft feathers around an owl's ears act like funnels for sound. The owl can move those feathers to help it pinpoint where a sound is coming from.
- Great Horned Owls often eat skunks, and their feathers and nest sites sometimes smell like one!

35

SNOWY OWL

Most of the time Snowy Owls are found in the Far North, where their white feathers can provide camouflage in the snow. But every few years, they suddenly appear much farther south than usual. This is because their favorite prey, the lemming, has periodic declines in its population. The owls are unable to find enough food, so they move south where they can find rodents and other animals to eat.

The rise and fall of the number of lemmings also affects the nesting pattern of Snowy Owls. They nest and raise young in years when lemmings are plentiful. In years when lemmings are scarce, Snowy Owls raise fewer chicks or may not nest at all.

Snowy Owls are large and powerful. They hunt during the day and find their prey by sight and sound.

Did You Know?

- Male Snowy Owls will defend their nests against almost any intruder, including wolves and foxes. Females are known to pretend to have a broken wing to lure intruders away from the nest.
- Geese and ducks sometimes nest near Snowy Owl nests for protection against Arctic Foxes.

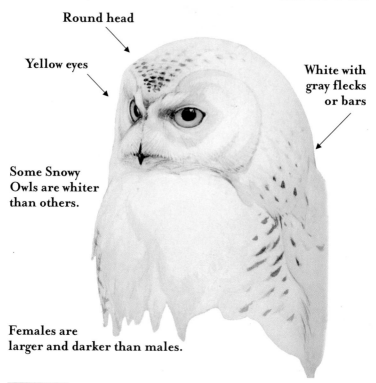

Round head

Yellow eyes

White with
gray flecks
or bars

Some Snowy
Owls are whiter
than others.

Females are
larger and darker than males.

Habitat During winter Snowy Owls can be found in the North in open country, including prairies, fields, marshes, beaches, and dunes. In summer these owls move north to the Arctic tundra.

Voice Snowy Owls are usually silent, except during nesting season when they are known to make a loud, repeated *krow-ow* while flying. They also sometimes make a repeated call that sounds like *rick*.

Food Small rodents, especially lemmings, are the main food for Snowy Owls, but they also hunt larger animals such as squirrels, rabbits, opossums, and skunks. They also hunt birds — sometimes large birds such as ducks or geese — snakes, lizards, frogs, insects, and scorpions.

BARN OWL

Do Barn Owls bring bad luck? Over the years some people have thought so. This may be because the Barn Owl's pale body gives it a ghostly look when it flies silently overhead in the moonlight. Or it may be that some people find its monkeylike face very frightening. Of course we now know that the only bad luck that they bring is for the rodents they are so good at catching.

Barn Owls are excellent hunters. They almost always hunt at night. Barn Owls fly low over the ground, watching and listening for prey. They often glide against the wind. This slows down their flight and allows them to find their prey more easily.

True to their name, Barn Owls often roost during the day in the dark shadows inside barns, but they also sleep in trees or caves. If one is discovered, it will stare at the intruder and sometimes weave its head back and forth in a kind of dancing motion.

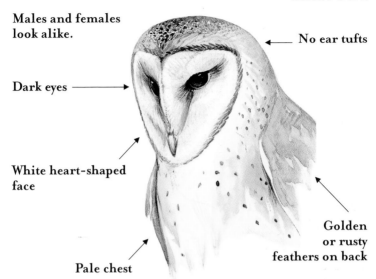

Males and females look alike.

No ear tufts

Dark eyes

White heart-shaped face

Pale chest

Golden or rusty feathers on back

Habitat Found all over the world, Barn Owls inhabit woodlands, marshes, prairies, and deserts. They hunt over open land and often live around farms.

Voice Barn Owls do not hoot like larger owls. They make a shrill rasping hiss or a snore that sounds like *kschh* or *shiiish*. They also make a loud shriek and a low growl that sounds like a large dog.

Did You Know?

• A Barn Owl's hearing is so good that it can find its prey in complete darkness.

• Barn Owls are such excellent hunters that they have been imported to Australia and New Guinea to hunt rodent pests.

• Like other owls, the Barn Owl's soft feathers make no noise when it flies.

Food Barn Owls usually prey on rodents, including voles, mice, and rats. They also hunt rabbits, shrews, and moles, and sometimes birds, insects, and lizards.

SHORT-EARED OWL

The Short-eared Owl is one of the few owls that often hunts during the day. It is most likely to be seen in the early morning or late afternoon. The Short-eared Owl most often uses its keen sense of hearing to detect and locate its prey. It flaps its wings and then glides very low over open ground. It will sometimes hover for a moment before pouncing on its prey or continuing onward. This uneven, flopping flight is one of the easiest ways to identify a Short-eared Owl.

The female Short-eared Owl builds a nest on the ground, concealed in weeds or under a bush. The nest is made out of dried grasses and lined with downy feathers. The young Short-eared Owls leave the nest about two weeks after they hatch, but before they can fly. They explore the area around the nest on foot for the next two weeks, after which they begin their first flights. This behavior may be a way to avoid predators since the nest is out in the open. The parents feed the young until they learn how to fly.

Small ear tufts are usually hard to see.

Dark patches call attention to the yellow eyes.

Habitat Short-eared Owls are found around prairies, marshes, dunes, and farmland. Most Short-eared Owls stay in one place throughout the year, but some migrate south. How far they travel is not known.

Did You Know?
- Short-eared Owls are about the size of a large crow.
- The territory of a single nesting pair of Short-eared Owls may stretch over 100 acres.
- The Short-eared Owl is found on many islands, including Hawaii.

Voice The call of a Short-eared Owl is a sneezy bark that sound like *kee-yow!* or *wow!* or *waow!*

Food Short-eared Owls prey mostly on small rodents, especially voles. They are also known to eat other small mammals, such as mice and lemmings, and small birds.

LONG-EARED OWL

The Long-eared Owl is one of the shiest birds. It spends its days hiding in dense cover. If its perch is disturbed, a Long-eared Owl raises its ear tufts and freezes in place, looking like a stubby tree branch.

The Long-eared Owl hunts at night and can sometimes be seen at dusk as it flies over fields getting ready for the night's hunting. Long-eared Owls sometimes hunt in groups, especially if there are plenty of rodents in an area.

Instead of building nests, Long-eared Owls use nests deserted by squirrels or other birds such as crows or hawks. If the owl's nest is disturbed, one parent may try to distract the intruder by pretending to be injured. It will call noisily and drag one wing along the ground in an imitation of a crippled bird. When the intruder goes after the parent, the owl quickly flies away. At other times a Long-eared Owl will raise its wings and make itself look as large and frightening as possible.

The long dark ear tufts are close together and stick up straight.

The Long-eared Owl is about the same size as a crow.

Streaks on the chest run lengthwise.

Habitat The Long-eared Owl is common in some areas with dense groves of trees. In drier areas it may perch in palm trees or in trees covered with vines. It hunts over open fields and meadows.

Voice The call of the Long-eared Owl is a low, moaning *hooooo*. It also makes a sound like a cat's meow.

Food Long-eared Owls eat mostly small rodents such as mice, rats, and gophers. Sometimes they hunt small birds or insects.

Did You Know?

- Long-eared Owls hunt by flying low over fields, crossing back and forth, then swooping down on their prey. They may also be seen hovering over a field.
- A Long-eared Owl can hear so well that it can catch mice tunneling under snow.

43

SCREECH-OWLS

In spite of its name, a screech-owl does not screech. During the day these small owls are very quiet. They

spend their time sleeping in holes in trees or in dense thickets. At night their call sounds more like a whinny or a whistle.

As night falls, screech-owls begin to hunt. Often they sit on a perch and watch and listen for their prey to pass. They have extremely good eyesight and hearing. Other times they cruise overhead, looking for food.

Two screech-owls are closely related. The Eastern Screech-Owl is found east of the Rocky Mountains. It is the only bright red-brown owl in the East that has ear tufts. The Western Screech-Owl is found west of the Rockies. It looks similar to the Eastern Screech-Owl, but their calls differ.

Did You Know?
• If you hear a screech-owl, you may be able to attract it by imitating its call.
• Screech-owls sometimes bathe at night in birdbaths.

SCREECH OWLS

Eastern Screech-Owl

Screech-owls are the only small owls with ear tufts.

Screech-owls can be either gray or red.

Males and females look alike.

Screech-owls are about the size of a robin.

Western Screech-Owl

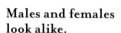**Habitat** Screech-owls are found in woods, groves, and in shade trees almost anywhere in the United States and Canada. They are often found in suburbs with woods or parks, in deserts, and in woods on the lower parts of mountains.

Voice The Eastern Screech-Owl makes a soft whinny or trilling sound that descends in pitch. The call of the Western Screech-Owl is a series of hollow whistles on one pitch. It has the rhythm of a small ball bouncing to a standstill.

Food Screech-owls hunt all kinds of small rodents, especially mice, shrews, and sometimes bats. They also eat a wide variety of beetles, moths, and spiders. Some even catch small fish.

BIRDS OF PREY IN FLIGHT

Eagles, hawks, Ospreys, and vultures often soar high above the ground looking for prey. These illustrations of birds in flight can help you decide which bird of prey you are seeing.

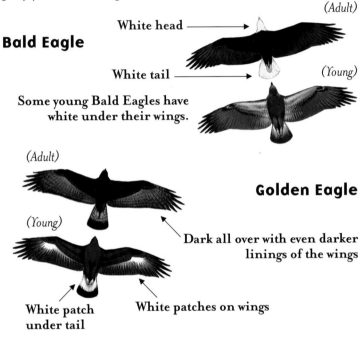

Bald Eagle

(Adult)

White head ⟶

White tail ⟶

(Young)

Some young Bald Eagles have white under their wings.

Golden Eagle

(Adult)

Dark all over with even darker linings of the wings

(Young)

White patch under tail

White patches on wings

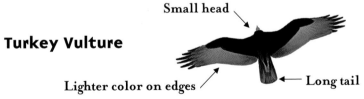

Turkey Vulture

Small head

Lighter color on edges

Long tail

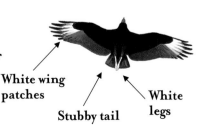

Black Vulture

Black Vultures are blacker than Turkey Vultures.

White wing patches

Stubby tail

White legs

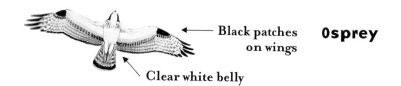

Black patches on wings → **Osprey**

Clear white belly

Red-tailed Hawk

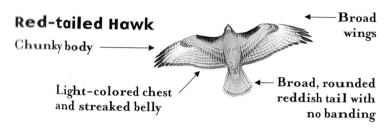

Chunky body →

Light-colored chest and streaked belly

Broad wings ←

Broad, rounded reddish tail with no banding ←

Northern Goshawk

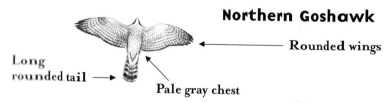

Rounded wings ←

Long rounded tail →

Pale gray chest

Northern Harrier

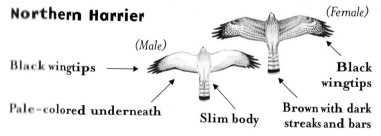

(Female)

(Male)

Black wingtips →

Pale-colored underneath

Slim body

Black wingtips

Brown with dark streaks and bars

Peregrine Falcon

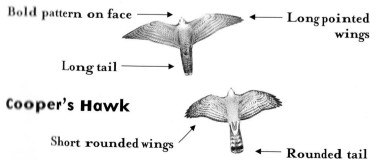

Bold pattern on face →

Long pointed wings ←

Long tail →

Cooper's Hawk

Short rounded wings →

Rounded tail ←

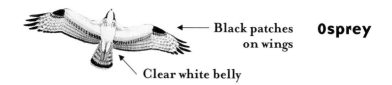

Black patches on wings → **Osprey**

Clear white belly

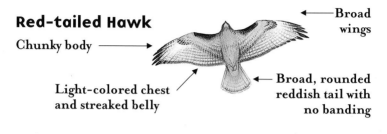

Red-tailed Hawk

Chunky body →

← Broad wings

Light-colored chest and streaked belly

← Broad, rounded reddish tail with no banding

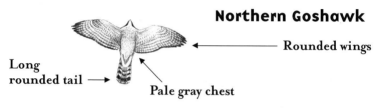

Northern Goshawk

Rounded wings

Long rounded tail →

Pale gray chest

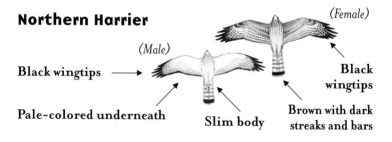

Northern Harrier

(Female)

(Male)

Black wingtips →

Pale-colored underneath

Slim body

Black wingtips

Brown with dark streaks and bars

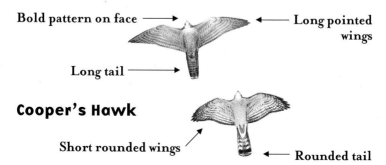

Peregrine Falcon

Bold pattern on face →

← Long pointed wings

Long tail →

Cooper's Hawk

Short rounded wings

← Rounded tail